# HMS ARK ROYAL

## THE SHIP
### AND
## HER MEN

**DAVID SMITH**
**AND**
**ANDREW WYNN**

MARITIME BOOKS

*First published in Great Britain in 1988*
*by Maritime Books, Liskeard, Cornwall.*

*ISBN 0 907771 39 4*

*Printed and bound in Great Britain by*
*Penwell Ltd., Callington, Cornwall*

# FOREWORD

## Humphrey T. Norrington

*Executive Director Overseas Operations*
*Barclays Bank PLC*

As a supporter of the King George's Fund for Sailors for over 70 years, it is a great privilege and pleasure for us to sponsor this fascinating publication which tells the story of the *Ark Royal* and her men.

It is perhaps particularly appropriate for Britain's leading global bank to be associated in this way with the premier ship of the Royal Navy, since Barclays Bank is represented in most of the countries which *Ark Royal* will visit as she sails around the world.

I am sure this book will give many a welcome insight into life on board this magnificent ship.

This book is dedicated
to the Men of HMS *Ark Royal*,
past, present and future.

# PREFACE

The authors of this book joined HMS *Ark Royal* in 1984 during the latter stages of building at Swan Hunters shipyard in Newcastle-upon-Tyne.

In the next two years the ship developed from a towering mass of steel seemingly tied forever to her fitting out berth by miles of lines, hoses and cables, to a fully effective and operationally capable warship.

The authors were Deputy Heads of the Air Engineering and Supply Departments. With their colleagues in the other departments and in the Squadrons, theirs was the responsibility for the day to day management of the ship throughout the highly complex programme necessary to bring ship, aircraft, machinery, equipment, weapons, stores and most important of all—the men, to the required state of readiness in the timescale allowed in the overall Fleet plan.

In April 1986 HMS *Ark Royal* passed her Operational Readiness Inspection and moved on to fulfil her progamme. The authors look back on their time on board with vivid memories of challenges faced, standards achieved, deadlines met, and with an awareness of the privilege of playing some small part in creating what HMS *Ark Royal* now is—one of the country's most capable and important projections of maritime power.

However, their most lasting memory will be of the ship's company and their achievements. The men of *Ark Royal* are the vital factor behind the ship's famous name. Without them, the ship would be nothing.

*Final approach.*

# CHAPTER ONE

# FLOATING AIRFIELD

As the helicopter flies out over the grey Atlantic waters, the ship on the murky horizon gradually takes shape. Its superstructure sits on the starboard side with an expanse of flat deck aft and to port. Closer, the eye discerns the identifying features of the Royal Navy's newest aircraft-carrier, HMS *Ark Royal*; two massive funnels carrying the exhaust of the four Rolls Royce Olympus marine gas turbines well clear of the flight deck; three masts, the taller topped by a constantly turning surface warning radar aerial placed at the highest point to give maximum coverage; a large radome at either end of the superstructure, concealing the aerials of the ship's powerful missile direction radars; an aircraft recovery crane with the jib tucked neatly away below the bridge; the twin-railed Sea Dart missile launcher, with a honeycomb structured efflux blast deflector protecting the people and equipment on the flight deck behind it; and the ugly but efficient ski-jump sloping above the otherwise aesthetic line of the bows.

The helicopter banks into the downwind leg, and an impression of the ship's size seizes the mind. This is not the 90,000 ton supercarrier of the United States Navy, but is nonetheless the largest Royal Navy warship afloat today. 20,000 tons of Tyneside crafted steel glides with seeming rocklike steadiness through the white-capped sea at 28 knots. From half a mile away all that betrays the huge forces propelling the ship is a plume of brown haze whirling horizontally from the funnels and a mountain of water rising from the stern, whipped to a froth by 100,000 shaft horsepower. Further details become visible flying down the port side; the Phalanx close-in weapon systems mounted in the eyes of the ship and on the sponson on the port quarter; a large, slowly revolving long range air warning radar atop the bridge; two pairs of satellite communications aerials; the White Ensign standing stiffly from the yardarm; two Harriers and three Sea Kings arrayed on the flight deck; flight deck tractors poised with towing bars ready, and scurrying human activity in different coloured surcoats each denoting different functions. White-painted markings blemished by black tyre streaks delineate the flight deck, along whose length runs a broad black line showing the fixed-wing runway; and a large white capital R for *Ark Royal* on the starboard quarter.

The pilot's right hand nudges the cyclic control column to the left, and the helicopter leans suddenly on its side with a protesting vibration felt through the airframe from the main rotor. Now it steadies and descends on final approach. A voice in the headset orders the pilot to hold his position astern of the ship. Surcoated figures scrabble around the undercarriage of one of the Sea Kings on the flight deck, then run crouched until clear of the rotor disc and stand in front of the aircraft holding aloft one, two, three, four nylon lashings. Safe to lift off, the Sea King's rotor disc angles up as collective pitch is applied, the oleos stretch and the 10 ton airframe teeters on the brink of flight. The tyres part company with the non-slip flight deck coating and the helicopter staggers heavily into the air away from the ship, feeling the weight of its two tons on fuel and the external load of depth-charges and Mark 46 torpedoes.

*All lashings removed, a Sea King is cleared to lift off.*

The headset speaks again, and the pilot guides the helicopter towards number 5 spot astern of the island. The rotor tips seem about to collide with the after radome looming large in the windscreen; the cockpit suddenly fills with the fumes of the ship's Olympus engines, and the aircraft rocks in the turbulence of the island's slipstream as it descends to an abrupt landing cushioned by the shock-absorbing undercarriage. The rotor noise changes as pitch is reduced while handlers run in to lash the helicopter to the deck. The fuel to the twin turbines is cut off, they run down and the headset goes dead, leaving a numbing silence and an awareness of the new motion of the flight deck slowly rising and falling.

*Opposite: Loading a depth charge onto an ASW Sea King.*

As the passenger disembarks from the aircraft to be guided into the ship through an access half way along the island, he steps carefully over the ringbolts set every few feet into the flight deck and the power cables and fuel lines already snaking their way out to the helicopter. He squeezes between the deflated radome of a parked airborne early warning Sea King and the superstructure, and pauses as a Sea Harrier positions itself for take-off 30 feet away from him. Seemingly impervious to the high-pitched whine of the idling Pegasus engine, a helmeted rating stoops away from the Harrier writing on a handheld blackboard the numbers and settings he is receiving on his loop headset from FlyCo; he turns and holds the blackboard up, bracing

11

himself against the 40 knot wind over the deck while the pilot injects the settings into his navigation computer. Satisfied, the pilot gives a thumbs-up, the FlyCo lights go to green, and the Pegasus engine winds up to the howl of maximum power. Nozzles pointing straight back, brakes selected off, and the Harrier accelerates down the runway. The nose wheel shock absorber takes the strain of meeting the start of the ski-jump at 60 knots, and the aircraft hurtles off the ramp at an angle of 12½°, the nozzles swivelled to give 30% lift and 70% forward thrust the instant the wheels lose contact with the flight deck. Nose-high, the Harrier gains speed while the pilot gradually adjusts the nozzle angle to trade engine-lift for wing-lift,

until after a few seconds the 9½ ton aircraft is in normal wingborne flight and rapidly accelerating. Its mission is Combat Air Patrol 100 miles down the threat sector from the ship.

\* \* \* \* \*

Flying operations from *Ark Royal*'s 600 feet long flight deck are the pivot of all activity throughout the ship. The ship's primary rôle is to deploy anti-submarine helicopters in support of a force at sea. *Ark Royal*'s anti-submarine capability is provided by 820 Squadron, which is formed of 9 Sea King helicopters, their crews, maintenance personnel, mobile support equipment and attached support staff. 820 Squadron's permanent

*A Sea Harrier takes flight.*

home is the Royal Naval Air Station at Culdrose in West Cornwall. Whenever *Ark Royal* returns to her base port at Portsmouth, the Squadron disembarks to Culdrose to carry on with maintenance, continue flying training and give some well-earned leave. The Sea Kings of 820 Squadron are the Mark 5 version carrying the latest updated sensors and avionic equipment in an airframe designed in the 1960s. The Westland/Augusta EH-101 helicopter will replace Sea Kings, but meanwhile these tried and proven aircraft are highly effective units equipped with radar, submersible sonar, passive sonar and associated contact analysis and processing equipment, as well as advanced com-

*Concentration. There is no room for error in aircraft maintenance.*

munications and threat warning electronics. To prosecute a submarine contact, Sea Kings can deploy homing torpedoes or depth charges, and normally operate in pairs or groups of three, or in cooperation with surface escorts or RAF Nimrod aircraft.

With their long endurance, Sea Kings are a formidable anti-submarine weapon platform. During the operational exercises that *Ark Royal* frequently takes part in with RN or NATO forces, 820 Squadron usually works a 'Ripple 3' system, whereby 3 Sea Kings are kept in the air and constantly on patrol. 'Ripple 3' can be sustained for very long periods and is the severest test of stamina and skill for aircrew and maintenance crews

*An Airborne Early Warning (AEW) Sea King with the radome rotated for take off/landing.*

*A Sea Harrier settles in the hover alongside the ship just before landing vertically.*

*Work progressing in the radar bay of a Sea Harrier in harbour.*

Below: *A Sea Harrier taxiing backwards into its alloted space.*

alike, typically working 10 hours on and 10 off, 7 days a week, week in and week out, whatever the weather. Constant training is necessary to keep aircrew in practice with their flying and operational skills; one mistake by them or by the maintenance crews on a dark, rough, freezing night after three weeks of operating at the limit of physical endurance can bring disaster.

820 Squadron's task is to locate and destroy hostile submarines well away from *Ark Royal* and the main force of ships. Should a submarine penetrate the screen however, it will be confronted with *Ark Royal*'s own sonar. *Ark Royal* herself is fitted with the latest and most powerful sonar in any surface ship, together with highly advanced computer assistance to identify contacts at medium range. Submarine Captains have had to learn a new respect in an area where once they had the undisputed advantage.

*Ark Royal*'s second Squadron is 801, equipped with 5 or more Mark I Sea Harriers, whose parent shore base is the Royal Naval Air Station at Yeovilton. These amazing aircraft are familiar to thousands of people who have seen them perform at air shows, demonstrating their ability to hover, manoeuvre up, down, sideways, backwards and forwards, 'bow' to the crowd and then stand on their tail and climb almost vertically into the sky in an unforgettable display of thrust and power. The Harriers and pilots of 801 Squadron, together with their main-

Armourers make ready a practice 1000lb. bomb before flight.

Right: *A Sea Harrier returning from Combat Air Patrol.*

tenance crews, 'won their spurs' whilst operating from HMS *Invincible* during the Falklands conflict of 1982.

The Sea Harrier (Shar) owes its extraordinary versatility to its system of vectored thrust. Instead of the power being directed straight astern as in most jet aircraft, the thrust of the Rolls Royce Pegasus turbofan is directed through four nozzles in the side of the fueslage. These nozzles can be swivelled from straight back, through 90° to the vertical, and a few degrees beyond the vertical to provide the ability to taxi backwards when manoeuvring on the ground, or even to brake in mid-air. In combat, the technique of vectoring in flight or 'viffing', has an extremely disconcerting effect on the pilot of an enemy aircraft setting itself up in a missile firing position astern of a Shar; for the

Shar can lose two or three hundred knots of speed very rapidly, so the pursuing aircraft has no choice but to overshoot and become the hunted instead of the hunter. Argentinian Daggers and Skyhawks found out about this the hard way; and in peacetime air combat exercises with foreign Air Forces, the Sea Harrier marks up an enviable success rate against far more powerful and sophisticated interceptors.

801 Squadron's main rôle with *Ark Royal* is to support the ship and other friendly maritime forces by maintaining a Combat Air Patrol. Operating, like the Sea Kings, to the limits of human and equipment performance, two Sea Harriers can be kept in the air for extended periods. Armed with Sidewinder 9L air-to-air missiles and twin 30mm Aden cannons, their task is to prevent unwanted

intruders from aproaching the force.

The second line of defence is *Ark Royal's* medium range Sea Dart surface-to-air missile system. Closer in, the Sea Gnat chaff dispensing system may be used to seduce the radar systems of incoming aircraft or missiles; and if all else fails the Phalanx Close In Weapon System will automatically shoot down any object approaching the ship above a certain speed unless it is switched off.

Sea Harriers are also highly effective in their secondary rôle of anti-ship strike; for this their armament is the highly effective Exocet-type Sea Eagle missile. A third rôle is conventional bombing, and a further capability is photographic reconnaissance.

A major shortcoming experienced by the Task Force during the Falklands conflict was the lack of airborne early warning, known as AEW. It was necessary at times to detach ships fitted with long range air warning radar on their own some way between the main force and the direction of the air threat. It was while acting as an air radar picket that HMS *Sheffield* was destroyed by an Exocet missile fired by an Argentinian Super Etendard.

The ubiquitous Sea King provided the answer, and in a remarkably short time in 1982 an AEW variant was developed, equipped with the radar from the RAF Nimrod aircraft. The AEW Sea Kings are operated by 849 Squadron, based at Culdrose. The three

*An ASW Seaking of 820 squadron prepares to land.*

projects below the fuselage to give all-round coverage; when the aircraft is on final approach for landing, the whole assembly is swivelled to lie alongside the fuselage.

The purpose of *Ark Royal*'s existence is to operate the aircraft of 820 and 801 Squadrons and 849 B Flight at sea. However *Ark Royal* has been designed and equipped to fulfil two further rôles. A most important capability is to provide the facilities for Command and Control of maritime forces. During exercises, and in war, *Ark Royal* is the flagship of Flag Officer Flotilla Three, who in addition to his national responsibilities is also a NATO Force Commander. The ship carries very advanced communications and message handling equipment, providing the Admiral and his staff with operational intelligence and the means to deploy maritime and air forces effectively.

*Ark Royal* is also capable of deploying amphibious units such as a force of Royal Marines or their equivalents from other NATO countries, and of supporting them with all their logistic requirements. Unlike the assault ships HMS *Intrepid* and *Fearless*, *Ark Royal* is not a purpose-built amphibious support ship; but by embarking 845 Commando Sea King Squadron instead of 820 and putting camp beds on every square foot of empty deck space in compartments and passageways, a 'quick dash' rôle can be fulfilled.

Each of the distinct rôles which together add up to *Ark Royal*'s overall capability has to be supported by countless functions which are the responsibility of the ship's departments. To name but a few, the Executive department operates the ship's weapons, mans the Operations Room and provides the seamanship skills required to take a ship to sea and carry out essential functions such as refuelling at sea or transferring stores from another ship by jackstay. The Marine Engineering Department provides an enormous range of support, from main propulsion to fresh water, from electricity generation and distribution to manufacturing liquid oxygen

*Replenishment of fuel from a Royal Fleet Auxiliary at night. A hose is passed to Ark Royal by heavy jackstay transfer and connected to the ship's refuelling system. Speed and efficiency are important because while the two ships are joined they are unable to take evasive action in the event of attack.*

aircraft of 849 B Flight are attached to *Ark Royal*, and their rôle is to keep one helicopter constantly on task, providing early warning to friendly forces of aircraft approaching at low level. They can also provide radar information to guide Harriers for intercepts of air contacts and provide a surface picture covering thousands of square miles.

The AEW Sea King is distinguishable from the anti-submarine version by an ungainly 'dustbin' attached to the right-hand side of the airframe. This dustbin is in fact an inflatable radome protecting the radar antenna. While the aircraft is in flight, the antenna for Harrier pilots to breathe. The Weapons Engineering Department maintains weapons, sensors, communications and computer equipment at operational readiness. The Supply Department feeds, clothes and pays the whole ship's company and maintains the huge inventory of stores and spare parts required by the ship and her squadrons. The Air Department is responsible for the safe and timely conduct of air operations, and for Air Traffic Control in the vicinity of the ship. The Air Engineering Department services, tests and repairs everything from a small component in a Harrier's Blue Fox radar to major parts of an airframe, and is responsible for the stowage and preparation of all air weapons. The Medical, Dental and Meteorology departments and the Chaplaincy also play important parts in the overall support provided by *Ark Royal* to her squadrons.

Whenever mention is made of this squadron or that department carrying out some complex task, which may need to be performed in atrocious weather conditions or employing technology which is at the leading edge in its field, it is impossible not to marvel at the impressive equipment fitted and used throughout the ship. To think no further would be to overlook the vital element of *Ark Royal*—and that is the 1200 men of the Royal Navy who man the ship and her squadrons.

*A weather forecast is prepared in the Meteorological Office, one of the few compartments to be fitted with a porthole.*

*Sea Eagle missiles being embarked.*

*Junior Officers under training assisting in moving a Sea Eagle missile during the embarkation of ammunition.*

# CHAPTER TWO

# THE SHIP

When each man joins HMS *Ark Royal* he is given a pocket map to help him find his way around the ship, because it takes some time to become familiar with the hundreds of passageways, compartments, ladders, lobbies and hatches within the ship. It is a warship's business to go looking for trouble in time of war, with the risk of sustaining damage in action. To minimise the spread of fire or flood, *Ark Royal* is divided both laterally and vertically into a number of watertight boxes, each watertight division itself contains further sub-divisions. Small wonder then that everyone on board has experienced at some time or other the frustrating feeling of wanting to get somewhere he knows he's seen once, but not knowing how to find it again.

Every passageway, compartment, door, hatch and even ventilation trunking in Royal Naval ships is identified with a 'damage control' marking. A compartment labelled, say 5G1 is on 5 deck, which is 4 decks below the flight deck; it is in 'Golf' section, which is the seventh watertight section of the ship starting from the bows; and it is on the starboard side. There are many other markings as well. Every pipe is labelled with what its function is, such as 'HP Air', or 'Domestic Hot', with an arrow indicating direction of flow. Doors and hatches may have a Z on them to indicate the boundary between two watertight divisions; or an A, which shows the boundary of the airtight 'citadel' used to prevent radioactive fallout or chemical agents from entering the ship. Throughout the ship there are arrows indicating the direction of escape, which glow in the dark in case of a total power failure. The only windows, or scuttles, in the ship are on the bridge, in the Aircraft Control Room, in the Admiral's quarters and (as a design afterthought) in the Meteorological Office so that the weather men are spared the embarrassment of forecasting imminent rain when in fact it's a glorious day. The ship's company is completely dependent on artificial lighting and therefore on uninterrupted power supplies. There are emergency lights throughout the ship; and since the Falklands campaign, there are also emergency breathing sets strategically placed so that personnel can escape from smoke-filled areas.

The importance of ship knowledge and of damage control measures is impressed on all newcomers to *Ark Royal*, and in a few weeks they can find their way about without a second thought.

Our visitor who arrived by helicopter in the midst of air operations on the flight deck is escorted into the island through a two door airlock, and into the Aircraft Control Room. A Warrant Officer is seated at a console fitted with communications to the Flying Control position adjacent to the bridge, known as FlyCo, and to the hangar and flight deck. Two closed circuit TV screens show the areas of the flight deck forward and aft of the island which cannot be seen through the ACR window, and magnetic markers on a board in front of the Warrant Officer show the exact position of every aircraft on the flight deck and in the hangar. Movements of aircraft on deck or between the flight deck and hangar can be planned with these markers, so that the Sea King or Harrier that is required for the next serial is always available—a complex task.

*A maintenance rating washes the compressor section of one of the two gas turbine engines fitted to a Sea King—in the fresh air, whilst . . .*

Down a ladder and directly below the ACR is the Hangar Control Position. An armoured window overlooks the gigantic hangar—as high as a two-storey house and nearly as long and as wide as the ship itself. Sea Harriers and Sea Kings are tethered with chain lashings in precise positions to make the most of the space available. A Harrier is being towed by a small electric tractor unit onto the after lift. The handling team check carefully that the Harrier is positioned exactly in the centre, the lift driver blows a whistle to warn personnel to stand clear, and an ear-piercing klaxon sounds as the lift ascends slowly towards the flight deck. Two vast hydraulic rams become visible, pushing outwards on the cantilever struts supporting the lift. After twenty seconds the Harrier reaches flight deck level and the lift becomes part of the runway surface, locked securely into place with huge hydraulic bolts. The klaxon ceases, leaving relative quiet, and work continues on the remaining aircraft. Right aft, an AEW Sea King stands on blocks while its undercarriage wheels are changed. Its five main rotor blades are folded neatly above the rear fuselage and the tail rotor pylon is also folded back on itself so as to take up the least space possible. Three ASW Sea Kings in various stages of maintenance are lined up directly below the Hangar Control Position window with only inches between each of them. At the front of the hangar, beyond the forward aircraft lift, a Harrier appears to be in a sorry state with its wing removed and placed on a nearby trestle. Maintainers manoeuvre an overhead hoist above the fuselage, preparing to lower a replacement Rolls Royce Pegasus into the engine bay. This Harrier's orginal engine had been damaged, possibly by ingesting debris while operating ashore; onboard constant efforts are made by all to reduce ''foreign object damage'' (FOD) by regular 'FOD plods', during which even the smallest piece of debris is picked up. In a few hours this aircraft will be given a tethered power run on the flight deck and after a test flight will then be reported fully operational.

The aircraft maintainers work around the clock to keep their aircraft serviceable in the face of never-ending defects which inevitably arise when sophisticated airframes and equipment are highly utilised. Exposure to the salt-laden atmosphere of the flight deck means that anti-corrosion measures must be constantly applied to preserve the airframes. Whether a defect is large or small, every maintenance operation is carried out and checked to the most stringent standard. One incorrectly secured clip can lead to engine failure; and a tool left inadvertently amongst control linkages can result in a ditched aircraft and aircrew lives placed at risk.

Casting an eye round the hangar gives some insight into the degree of complexity of ship design necessary in an aircraft carrier. Workshops and ready-use storerooms are conveniently located on either side. Apart from the two huge aircraft lifts, eight other lifts give access to the hangar from the bowels of the ship. Bombs, missiles and torpedoes can be delivered to the hangar, or to the flight deck, from the magazines deep below the waterline. Food and stores can be sent directly to the correct storerooms, and even the ship's main Olympus engines can be moved to the hangar and thence to the flight deck after they have been replaced. The weapon lift can fulfil a secondary rôle by using an optional stop in the Sick Bay, so that casualties can be taken below from the flight deck or hangar without having to negotiate ladders and hatches.

A place for everthing, and everything in its place —the sides of the hangar are lined with containers of stores needed for the aircraft; there are special stowages for spare rotor blades for the Sea Kings, too bulky to keep down below in the main Air Storerooms. There is a stowage for a spare Sea Harrier tailplane on the bulkhead by the forward air-craft lift. When the tailplane is needed, the lift stops halfway to the flight deck, the tailplane is taken down, and down comes the lift to the waiting aircraft. Simple—but the result of careful planning by the ship's

*. . .in the hangar another aircraft maintainer prepares a main rotor head for fitting to a Sea King—in high temperatures and uncomfortable humidity.*

designers. Even the deckhead is used to advantage; it is criss-crossed with rails for overhead hoists for lifting heavy equipment to almost any point in the hangar, and fuel drop-tanks for the Harriers are kept high aloft and out of the way until they need to be fitted to the Harriers to give them extra range.

A single huge compartment in a ship, such as the hangar, can be a source of danger. Being above the waterline flood is not the first worry— but the risk of fire certainly is. The hangar is therefore fitted with a very powerful sprinkler system, which can deluge the area with water if a fire starts that cannot be extinguished immediately with 'first aid' appliances. Drenching in corrosive salt water may not do the aircraft any good, but better that than a fire quickly spreading throughout the ship. The hangar can also be sub-divided by two fire-curtains to prevent fire and smoke from spreading; nevertheless, aircraft with fuel in their tanks obviously require special care, which is one of the responsibilities of the ratings manning the Hangar Control Position. Their reactions can make the difference between an incident and a catastrophe.

The Hangar Control Position opens into 2 deck starboard passageway, which runs right around the ship beneath the flight deck. All newcomers are at once struck by the brightness of the white paintwork and blue polished tiles. Ship cleanliness is a major headache. Every single space in the ship 'belongs' to a Department. A small label on the bulkhead shows that this passageway is the property of 820 Squadron, and it names the Senior Rating who is responsible for its upkeep. The Senior Rating can allocate a number of ratings to keep the passageway up to the standard required, but he has to balance this task against his men's primary duties of handling or maintaining aircraft. In fact this passageway was swept and polished by a Naval Airman early this morning, shortly before completing his 10 hour watch on the flight deck. It may look clean to the visitor's untrained eye, but those paint splashes on the overhead cables, and the surplus grease on the door hinges will have to be removed before Captain's Rounds. Emphasis is not placed on ship husbandry for its own sake; this ship must be kept in good condition in order for it to stay in service for the next 25 or 30 years.

The Petty Officer on duty in the Safety Equipment room takes charge of the visitor's immersion suit, lifejacket and helmet. Here he and his team look after and maintain the life-preserving equipment of all the aircrew. His skills and attention to routine, detailed checks have been tested and found not wanting; there are several aircrew on board who have been recovered from ditched aircraft and are thankful that their ejection seat, parachute, lifejacket, dinghy and radio beacon worked when it mattered.

Further aft along 2 deck is the officer's accommodation. The visitor is shown to the cabin he will occupy for his stay on board. It is a box about 8 by 10 by 7 feet high, and it is comparative luxury, for he is not sharing with anyone else. It has a pull down sofa-bunk, wardrobe, two banks of drawers, a concealed sink with hot and cold water, and a desk. The officers would like to have a private meeting with the man who designed the 23-inch wide bunk, which in a rough sea is liable to fold up —with them trapped inside it.

Signs on other cabin doors such as 'Do Not Disturb—Ripple 3' show that the occupants are, for the duration of the exercise, living on a timetable linked to the cycle of Anti-Submarine flying operations: Briefs before flying, flying, sleeping and snatching a meal in the 24 hour Aircrew Refreshment Bar when a moment can be found. How they manage is a mystery, for here, even seven decks above the screws driving the ship at 28 knots, every fitting is vibrating; conversation, let alone sleep, is difficult. Added to which a Sea Harrier can be heard nearing the ship on its landing approach; as it slows to a hover at full power beside the ship, then moves over the deck and thumps down on its landing

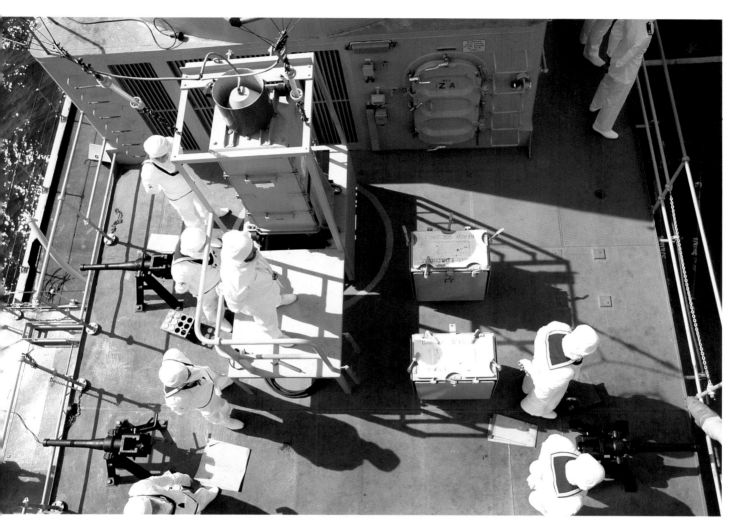

*The Ceremonial Guns Crew stands ready to fire a salvo on entering a foreign port.*

*Approaching Fort Lauderdale in Florida at procedure 'Alpha'—the flight deck ringed by smart sailors and the aircraft neatly lined up.*

spot six feet above the occupants of the cabins, the scream from the engine intakes and load roar from the exhaust are enough to wake the dead. Even *Ark*'s slumbering officers are disturbed momentarily.

In the Wardroom Anteroom three decks down, several officers are having a pre-lunch drink in front of the well stocked bar manned by a Steward. Most of them are holding soft drinks, observing a voluntary rule of abstinence from alcohol while at sea. Some are due to go on watch after lunch, while others are well aware that unexpected incidents can arise at any time. The Anteroom is a large compartment with seating space for 60, about a third of the officers carried during an exercise. The eating area, or Wardroom proper, is opposite the Anteroom. It is served by its own galley with a Petty Officer Cook in charge of a team of Cooks who provide the officers with 4 main meals a day, including a

cross between dinner and breakfast from midnight to 1am for those going on or coming off watch. There are two or three choices at each meal, served by Stewards. Healthy eating rules in this ship; chips are banned by the Supply Commander except, grudgingly, on Fridays with fish. None of the officers looks underfed, and they all speak well of the standard of food after making sure the Catering Officer is not within earshot.

Lunch over, the visitor is taken on a tour of the key areas of the ship. It starts along the port side passageway on 5 deck, which like 2 deck runs right round the ship and is the busiest thoroughfare on board. On the way to the Operations Room there are two Fire and Repair Party Posts painted red, which contain equipment needed to tackle fire, flood, hull damage and damage to electricity supplies. These posts are permanently manned by damage control teams at the

*A visitor is shown Aircraft Contol Position in the Operations Room.*

higher states of readiness and risk.

The first impression of the Operations Room or 'gloom room', is a dimly lit compartment crammed with radar displays and keyboards manned by about twenty officers and ratings wearing headsets. Each of them is intent on the computer display in front of him and is quietly talking into the boom microphone attached to his headset. The layout of the Operations Room is very carefully designed to enable the vast quantity of information that comes in to be analysed, filtered, assessed and reacted to without delay. The electronic heart of the process is a computer situated in another compartment, which can keep track of hundreds of contacts and allows information from one display to be selected and transferred to another.

Consoles around the perimeter of the Ops Room are dedicated to electronic warfare, the Sea Dart missile system, the Phalanx Close In Weapon System, data links from other ships or aircraft, and Sonar. Along one entire side is an array of consoles for Air Traffic, Helicopter and Fighter Controllers. In the centre are four tables whose surface is a large, circular display with a radar picture mixed with computer generated information. One of these tables is used by the Admiral and his staff to monitor the overall tactical picture; a second provides shipping and anti-collision information to the Officer of the Watch on the bridge; the other two are dedicated to the Sub-Surface and Above Water tactical pictures. In overall charge is an Advanced Warfare Officer, responsible for the proper flow of information and for giving tactical advice to the Captain, whose own console is at the hub of the Operations Room. In the Captain's absence the AWO is personally authorised to make immediate responses to a threat to the ship or the force on his own initiative.

At Action Stations the Ops Room is manned by sixty officers and ratings, including the Captain with his 'first eleven' of tactical experts, as well as damage control adviser who will allocate priorities for repair teams if the ship is hit. An efficient Operations Room is completely dependent on correct actions being taken by every member of the team—from Able Seaman to Captain. Training for all levels starts at the School of Maritime Operations at HMS *Dryad* near Portsmouth, but there is no substitute for constant practice at sea in organised exercises, with the occasional bonus of real (rather than simulated) Russian naval and air contacts. During such exercises the Ops Room is manned in 'Defence Watches', whereby officers and ratings of the Operations Branch work six hours on and six hours off continuously. By the end of the exercise they may not have seen daylight for some weeks, and they will certainly be more than ready for an uninterrupted night's sleep.

The Ops Room equipment itself is extremely complex. It is the responsibility of the Weapons Engineering Department to maintain every item in perfect condition and ready for action. Not only the Ops Room equipment, but also the sensors which feed information into it such as the several radar and sonar sets, and the weapons systems which are controlled from the Ops Room, must all be kept on top line. The Weapons Engineering Commander's department consists of eighty officers and ratings who have a non-stop task of planned maintenance and trouble-shooting. Among them are a number of highly skilled Artificers who can trace and repair faults in the smallest component of a computer, fire control radar or any other piece of advanced technology equipment.

Adjacent to the Operations Room is the Main Communications Office, equipped with a wide range of transmitters and receivers for external communications on frequencies ranging from HF to Super High Frequency. All non-aircraft communicatons to and from the ship are channelled via one of the two satellite systems, which provide the facility for nearly instantaneous worldwide communications. Apart from the voice traffic between nearby ships and aircraft, all signals are encrypted automatically before being transmitted; similarly, incoming signals are decrypted by machines whose code settings are changed daily at a certain time, so that all ships reading signals on a particular 'broadcast' are able to decipher the traffic they need to read. The most sensitive and highly classified signals are treated with two ciphers—firstly using code settings available only to a handful of officers or senior ratings, and then again using the normal daily cipher.

The MCO operates 24 hours a day, 365 days a year, regardless of whether the ship is in harbour or at sea. At peak periods in an exercise the MCO handles hundreds of signals a day. There would certainly be too many for the Radio Operators to handle them all individually, so signals in *Ark* are routed by an automatic system to whichever department needs to see them. A number of signal 'tails' are disposed in certain key areas of the ship, so that for example any signal which the Marine Engineering department needs to know about will be routed by the automatic message handling equipment to a teleprinter in the ME department office one deck below the MCO. If a signal is received that has an 'Immediate' prefix, a Radio Operator will spot it on a display in the MCO, alert the supervisor with a call of "Immediate on the tail", and the supervisor will see that a copy of that signal is delivered by hand to whichever officer needs to take immediate action on it.

Besides the Radio Operators who man the MCO there are also Tactical ROs, who keep watch on voice circuits on the bridge and

pass messages by flag hoist from the yard-arms or by Morse Code using the signal projectors on the bridge roof. The more senior RO(T)s, or Yeomen, are occasionally to be seen exchanging their own private messages to their opposite numbers on nearby ships using semaphore. Despite the wealth of advanced, worldwide communications equipment packed into the MCO, these older methods of passing mesages between ships still have their place in today's Navy, particularly when a policy of radio silence is in force so as not to give away *Ark Royal*'s position to enemy ships, or aircraft and satellites passing overhead.

Down below in the Ship Control Centre (SCC) on 6 Deck, the revolutions order indicator clicks repeatedly, settling finally on 120 r.p.m. Flying has finished temporarily; the Officer of the Watch has turned the ship

*The Ship Control Centre. Because the ship is at Action Stations the Engineer Officer of the Watch and his men are wearing anti-flash gloves and hoods.*

back onto the base course and ordered a reduction in speed. One of the Marine Engineering Mechanics on watch at the main engine control panel presses a button which sounds a bell at the Quartermaster's position on the bridge, nine decks higher, acknowledging the order. Both MEMs ease back on a lever on their console, which by a series of remote control linkages reduces the flow of fuel to the four Olympus gas turbines that have been driving the ship through the water at 28 knots. It is quiet in the SCC. Gone are the days of standing in the boiler-room footplates in an atmosphere of steam, oil and noise. *Ark Royal's* main machinery, and much of the auxiliary machinery, is controlled from the air-conditioned quiet of the SCC. A computer constantly monitors machinery performance by reading hundreds of sensors which feed in information of temperatures, pressues, fuel flows, revolutions and all manner of other data. The moment an abnormal reading is detected, an alarm sounds and a written description of the fault runs off a printer.

Although the engines can be operated for long periods without any personnel in the engineering spaces, rounds are nevertheless carried out regularly as a 'Mark 1 Eyeball' double check of the automatic fault finding systems. However when the ship is closed down into its gastight condition there is no need for personnel to leave the safety of the SCC.

The Engineer Officer of the Watch sits at a desk behind the control console. He scans the dials in front of him to see for himself that the readings taken from the main engines and gearboxes are changing as he would expect with the reduction in revolutions. He speaks on an internal telephone with the Officer of the Watch, and they agree that as high speed is unlikely to be needed again for a few hours, two of the four Olympus engines can be shut down. At full power *Ark's* engines consume seven gallons of fuel per yard, so no opportunity is missed to use the most economical power combination that is compatible with the operational situation. In this case, to drive each shaft with one engine instead of two will save several tons of fuel and, just as important, will save running hours on the Olympus. The main engines have to be changed after a certain number of hours; spare Olympus engines are carried on board and can be changed at sea if absolutely necessary, but clearly it is prudent to shut engines down if they are not needed.

Besides, one of the Olympus engines— 'SIG' (**S**tarboard **I**nner **G**as turbine)—needs an item of planned maintenance carried out on it, so SIG and POG (Port Outer Gas turbine) are shut down, leaving SOG and PIG (Starboard Outer and Port Inner) driving the ship at a comfortable 16 knots. When SIG has cooled down, an Artificer will enter the engine module to carry out the necessary work. Each Olympus, as well as each of the eight diesel generators which supply electrical power for the ship, is housed in its own box, or 'module'. These modules absorb noise and are mounted on 'rafts', so that the very minimum amount of noise from running machinery is transmitted through the hull into the sea. This and other classified measures make it much harder for submarines, even with their highly sensitive sonars, to detect *Ark Royal* from a long distance.

Before entering SIG's module the artificer will have to disarm the device which automatically fills it with inert gas if the Olympus catches fire. The gas would be fatal to anyone working inside if accidentally activated. When he turns the key on the outside of the module an alarm sounds in the SCC to warn the Engineering Officer of the Watch that this first line of defence against fire is out of action. Like the hangar, the four huge compartments for which the Marine Engineers are responsible—two engine rooms and two gear rooms— have elaborate fire-fighting devices. For example if a fire in an Olympus module is not extinguished by the gas mechanism, the entire compartment can be filled with another type of inert gas; and if that fails, the engine room can be filled with foam.

The gear rooms each contain a gigantic gearbox, the size of a semi-detached house, which is needed to convert the high speed of the Olympus gas turbines into the relatively slow revolutions required on the propeller shafts. It was one of these gearboxes which exploded in *Ark*'s sister ship, HMS *Illustrious*, and caused a serious fire shortly after sailing from Portsmouth on a round-the-world deployment a few years ago. The fire took several hours to extinguish, and resulted in two months back in Portsmouth for repairs. *Ark*'s Ship Control Centre watchkeepers know that a potentially catastrophic incident can arise at any moment, and that their actions in the first few seconds can make the difference between minor damage or, at the other extreme, losing the ship.

Also in the SCC is the control position for the electricity supply for the whole ship. *Ark* has six Paxman Valenta diesel generators in the main machinery spaces and a further two located high above the waterline so that they can continue to provide vital electricity even if the ship is severely damaged. These generators are basically the same engines that power British Rail HS125 Inter City trains. Their combined power output is 12 megawatts, enough to supply a small town. There are seven main switchboards, through which is distributed power at several different voltages to, amongst other things, 20,000 lights and 500 motors. A significant degree of redundancy is designed into *Ark*'s electrical arteries; for example, all important electrical machinery, such as the pumps that maintain pressure in the saltwater firemain, take their power from one switchboard, and if the generator supplying that switchboard fails, a changeover switch will instantly take supplies from an alternative source. In addition, power can be supplied directly to an important piece of equipment. Some items, such as the gyros, are also provided with battery back-up.

Many other services are monitored and

*The Quartermaster at the steering position on the bridge. The ship's wheel is a thing of the past.*

controlled from the SCC, including air-conditioning, cooling water for radar sets and the Ops Room computer, hydraulics for the aircraft lifts, fresh water distilling plants and many, many others. The lights will only go out when the ship is paid off in about twenty years time.

On the bridge ten decks above the Ship Control Centre the Officer of the Watch replaces the handset of the internal telephone after authorising the two Olympus engines to be shut down. He checks the gyro compass repeater on the console at the front of the bridge to ensure that the Quartermaster has steadied the ship on the course he has ordered. He looks ahead through the armoured glass windows, out over the forward 909 radome, the 'graveyard' (a space on the flight deck is kept free for aircraft which develop a defect and have to be moved to one side to clear the deck for operational aircraft), the Sea Dart missile launcher and, right in the eyes of the ship, the Phalanx mounting. He is responsible for the safety of the ship for the duration of his watch, and has had to prove his competence to deal with the routine and the unforeseen before being entrusted with the ship.

On his right the Quartermaster sits at his console watching the rudder angle indicator as the autopilot gyro senses minute deflections from the course set and steers to compensate. The wheelhouse located deep in the ship is a thing of the past; instead the QM has a small control column to use if manual steering is required.

On the starboard side the Radio Operator handles any signals which are directed to the bridge and keeps watch on the voice circuits patched through from the MCO. The Bosun's Mate sits at his desk ready to act as messenger/telephone operator with a complex array of internal communications equipment available to him.

Consoles in front of the Officer of the Watch provide him with a variety of information. As well as the dials one might expect to find, showing the ship's course and speed and the engine telegraph and revolutions repeater, there are some rather more specialised indicators; for example indicators showing the depth of the towed torpedo decoy, and the direction of an approaching torpedo to enable the correct countermeasures to be taken. The elevation and bearing of the SCOT satellite aerials and of the 909 missile direction radars need to be monitored because their powerful microwave energy will harm aircrew if they fly through their beams at close range. There are 'Check Fire' alarm buttons to be used if it is necessary to order weapons to cease firing immediately. There is also an important looking button with a guard across it. A home made label underneath it, obviously composed by the Navigating Officer after one or two accidental activations, reads: "Magic Button. If pressed—Captain appears". This is the Captain's Call, used only if the OOW needs the Captain to come to the bridge instantly and does not have the time to explain why—a rarely used facility.

The most important dial on this bridge is the relative wind speed and direction indicator. Flying operations are completely dependent on wind over the deck being within prescribed limits for the launch or recovery of the different types of aircraft, or for folding the main rotors blades of a Sea King. Too much wind, and the blades will be damaged; too little wind, and on leaving the ski-jump a Harrier will sink gracefully, but expensively, into the sea instead of flying. From this dial, and knowing the ship's course and speed, the OOW can calculate the true wind speed and direction and waste no time in coming to a flying course when required.

Satisfied that the ship is on a safe course for the moment, the Officer of the Watch turns his attention to the chart table behind him to make sure that the young Second Officer of the Watch has noted the change in engine configuration in the ship's log. The OOW2 has done so and is now updating the ship's position on the chart from the Ship's Inertial

*The Captain reads signals brought to him on the bridge by the Chief Yeoman.*

Navigation System (SINS) and adding dead reckoning positions based on the new course and speed. SINS is a navigational aid originally developed to allow nuclear submarines to navigate safely while submerged and also to provide extremely accurate positional data for launching ballistic missiles. As well as SINS, *Ark Royal* is fitted with a satellite navigation system and the Decca and OMEGA systems. Nevertheless Seaman Officers have also to qualify in astro-navigation; and on a coastal passage, visual and radar fixes are made every few minutes to check on the accuracy of the electronic systems. With more than £300,000,000 worth of ship and aircraft, and 1200 lives in his hands, the Officer of the Watch leaves nothing to chance.

The Captain is on the bridge in his chair on the port side of the bridge. With him is his Second-in-Command (the Commander) dis-cussing a 'welfare' case. A signal has been received informing the ship that a rating's son is critically ill and advising that he should be landed at the earliest opportunity. The Captain decides that the rating should be transferred to the accompanying Royal Fleet Auxiliary storeship after the next replenishment; the RFA will then be detached to make for the Shetland Isles, and when within helicopter range the sailor will be flown to Sumburgh and on by commercial airline to London. The Commander leaves to tell the rating's Divisional Officer of the Captain's decision; the necessary signals will be made, and the rating will be at his son's bedside in 36 hours.

The Captain's Action Station is in the Operations Room; however he is content to leave the conduct of a routine exercise serial to the Advanced Warfare Officer (AWO) on watch, receiving regular reports on the bridge or in his sea-cabin a few paces away. The AWO is responsible for the tactical responses of the ship and for giving manoeuvring instructions to the OOW, who will carry them out provided the safety of the ship is not compromised. Both of them know exactly what decisions the Captain wishes them to take on their own initiative, and when they must consult him before taking any action—day or night. The ship's Heads of Department develop a sixth sense for when the Captain will have time to listen to the most important of the hundred and one daily occurrences affecting men, material or organisation, and come to the bridge to choose their moment for a slice of his time.

There is a constant flow of information between this Operations Room and the Bridge, and in the case of an aircraft-carrier there is a third vital link in the chain—the flying control position. Flyco is the shipborne equivalent to an airfield control tower; it is adjacent to the bridge and juts out over the flight deck giving a clear view forward and aft. The two most comfortable chairs in the ship are mounted on swivels close to the windows, and from them Lieutenant Commander (Flying) directs air operations, supervised by Commander (Air). His assistant is a rating (known as FlyCo 'logger') seated at a nearby console. Liaising with the Operations Room and the Officer of the Watch, the FlyCo team is responsible for implementing the day's flying programme, which has been planned to be compatible with the other exercise serials, but which seldom goes according to plan because of unforeseen commitments, defects and aircraft emergences. Lieutenant Commander (Flying), or 'Little F' as he is invariably

*The Commander, responsible for discipline on board, takes his turn in the stocks at a charity fun-raising 'village fête' held on the flight deck on passage across the Atlantic.*

known, allocates landing and take-off spots, orders aircraft movements, start-ups and shut-downs if, and only if, wind conditions are in limits, and throughout the day and night he or his Deputy juggle an intricate web of incompatible constraints to keep the aircraft flying safely to and from the small, wet, moving deck.

It is only too easy for an Officer of the Watch to order a course alteration just as a Sea King is about to touch down on the after end of the flight deck, or as weapon handlers are winching up a 1000 lb bomb onto a Harrier wing pylon. Little Fs are traditionally well versed in verbal invective—but it is just as easy for him to require an alteration of course at the worst possible moment for the OOW, as the latter is carefully weaving his

way through a pattern of ship contacts on the radar in low visibility. Just as pilots require constant practice to keep their flying skills honed, so also the bridge, FlyCo and Ops Rooms teams need to exercise their arcane skills regualrly to provide safe conditions for aircrew and aircraft. If emergencies happen —which they do—the correct reactions are made, instinctively, but only as a result of intensive training and thorough understanding of aircraft carrier operations. When an ASW Sea King ditched close astern of the ship one day, another helicopter launched, winched all the Sea King aircrew out of the sea and deposited them back on deck—all within 9 minutes.

That's teamwork!

*The aircrew of an ASW Sea King are winched from the sea after ditching. The tail wheel and the tip of the main rotor blade are still visible; but the aircraft sank before flotation bags could be attached.*

# CHAPTER THREE

# BEHIND THE SCENES

*Empty pallets are returned to the Royal Fleet Auxiliary* Resource *by helicopter during replenishment of provisions at sea.*

All the time that operations are being conducted in the Ops Room or on the Flight Deck, so also countless other activities are undertaken day and night throughout the ship. Some do not have the appeal of aviation and operations; for example maintenance of the ship's sewage treatment plants is not exactly first on the list for visiting VIPs to see.

However members of the ship's company who perform the supporting activities know very well that without their efforts and skills, *Ark Royal* would not continue to be operational for long.

In the depths of the ship a Petty Officer is carrying out magazine rounds. Explosives safety is taken very seriously, and all am-

*Preparation of the 100 loaves of bread made before breakfast every day in the ship's bakery.*

*Food—and plenty of it. Marines of the Royal Netherlands Marine Corps, embarked for an exercise, queue at the Junior Rates' servery.*

*Great importance is attached to maintaining high standards of hygiene in food service areas. Wardroom galley Cooks prepare for Captain's Rounds. Even the overhead light diffusers are taken down for the insides to be cleaned.*

munition stowages are visited regularly to check temperature and security. The Petty Officer unlocks the magazine with the keys he has signed for and swings open the heavy watertight door. The torpedo magazine gleams with clean paint and is sufficiently spacious for the weapons to be manoeuvred to and from their racks on specially designed trolleys. The deckhead is criss-crossed with lifting frames which are used for hoisting the torpedoes into the second or third tier racks. In one corner of the magazine is an access to the weapon lift, which is used to deliver ordnance to the flight deck and thence to the aircraft. The Petty Officer checks that no torpedoes have worked loose in their racks through the motion of the ship, casts his eye around to ensure there are no unsecured items or patches of liquid on the deck, and before leaving notes the highest and lowest temperatures shown by the thermometer since the last inspection.

It does not need much imagination to work out that if the weapon lift breaks down, torpedoes cannot be delivered to helicopters on the flight deck and submarines cannot be sunk. Maintenance of 'outside machinery' is one of the responsibilities of the Marine Engineering department. In an office on 6 deck in Lima Section (abbreviated to 6L), a Warrant Officer presides over a mass of wall charts, files, drawings and maintenance schedules. An elaborate bring-up system indicates when any item of equipment in the ship, from radar set to lift motor, is due to have planned maintenance carried out on it. The philosophy is to prevent defects by mending them before they arise; but of course unplanned defects can, and do, occur. When they do, the 'user' department raises a job card, which serves as a request for rectification and also as a source of information which can lead to the planned maintenance schedule being altered to prevent the defect recurring. The Warrant Officer allocates priorities to the job cards to fit as best as he can both the urgency of the defect and the resources he has to mend it.

Right now, top of the heap is the provisions vertiflo hoist, which the Catering Officer has reported unserviceable, with an added note that tomorrow's replenishment will be so much easier if it is mended today. It will be.

At that moment the Catering Officer and his Chief Petty Officer are in the Provision Room flat in 7P, where work has been going on in readiness for the next day's delivery of provisions from the accompanying Royal Fleet Auxiliary. The Caterers have two main concerns: one is to provide good food, and plenty of it, to feed 1200 men four times a day within a set financial allowance; the other is never to go below the minimum peacetime stock levels. Seven different provisions rooms open off this flat, of which four are refrigerated at different temperatures ranging from cool to deep freeze by machinery running constantly one deck below. Space is at a premium, so after completing issues to the galley both for today and tomorrow, the small catering staff have been bringing forward the old stock and making room for the sixty tons of dry and frozen provisions which they have ordered from the storeship.

Two decks above in the Main Galley, the Petty Officer Cook looks at the clock. It is 1130; time for afternoon watchkeeper's lunch. He gives the order to raise the shutters on the servery counters, and lunch begins. The junior ratings queuing in the dining hall are presented with a choice of three hot dishes, or a grill to order, or a salad, plus a pudding. The same is available to the Petty Officers and Chief Petty Officers waiting at the serveries in their respective dining-halls at the other side of the galley. Lunch will continue to be served until 1300, and after the whole ship's company has been through, the PO Cook and his watch of Cooks start all over again to produce supper. Never ending, and not many thanks (though there are a few who like what they eat and say so).

With a daily throughput of over 3000 people, management of the dining-halls is a large task in itself. The dining-hall party—a group of ratings from all departments—is

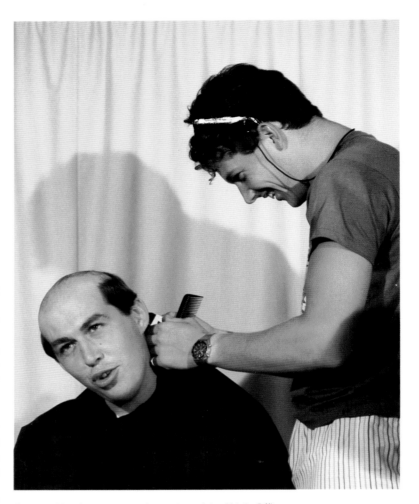

*Sponsored head shave! A Leading writer of the Ship's Office raises money for a ship's charity.*

responsible for setting up before meals, clearing away afterwards and washing the cutlery and crockery in the 'potwash' compartment—which at peak times is like a swamp of leftovers, swirling water and steam. Great importance is placed on maintaining a high standard of hygiene. As in the galley, there is plenty of opportunity for less than thorough work to lead to food poisoning with drastic effects on the ship's operational efficiency; but it has not happened yet, and the idea is to keep it that way.

*The Chinese laundrymen.*

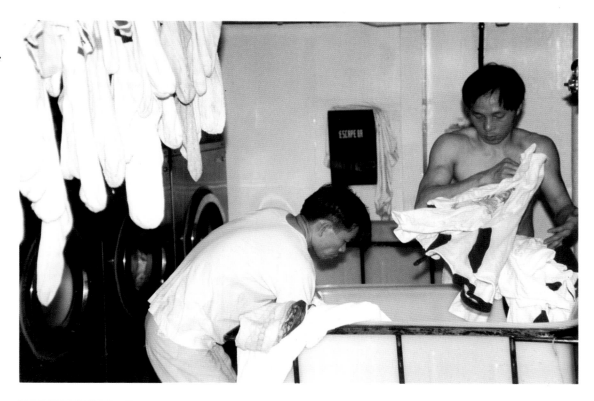

*"Tap Tap", the Chinese cobbler.*

The NAAFI Manager is doing brisk business forward in the Canteen in 5G Starboard. The daily beer allowance has already been issued to messdecks (and paid for). The ship's company can top up with soft drinks, sweets and chocolate ('nutty'), and buy anything from bootlaces to washing powder ('dhoby dust'), or from sweatshirts to stereos from the gift shop in 7E. There is also a shop where duty-free tobacco and cigarettes can be bought on production of coupons which at the end of the month are strictly accounted for to HM Customs and Excise. The manager and his assistants are civilians, but at Action Stations are trained members of the ship's first-aid teams. NAAFI is a non-profit making organisation which returns a percentage of its proceeds to the ship and to naval charities. These initials stand for Navy, Army and Air Force Institute (not—as the manager was overheard informing a lady guest of the Chief Petty Officers' Mess in New York—Naval Air Arm Flying Instructor).

Although sailors do some of their own dhobying, most is done in the ship's laundry manned by a Hong Kong Chinese contractor. *Ark Royal*'s contract is let to the Shao brothers, who with their crew of laundrymen provide a same day service to the whole ship's company from their premises in 3C. Washing, pressing and sorting goes on nearly continuously, and in addition very high quality bespoke uniforms, suits and shoes are made on board by the Chinese tailor and cobbler working in cramped and improvised spaces. As often as not one of the laundrymen is to be found stirring a bubbling saucepan which will turn out to be a finely prepared Chinese dish.

Right aft on the quarterdeck the ship's two Physical Training Instructors run a keep fit session during the lunch hour. Many of the ship's company take the opportunity of a break in their duties to pursue physical recreation, either in organised sessions, by running laps of the flight deck if there is no flying, or by doing circuits in the ship's gym. The gym used to be an empty compartment

*Cookery—Chinese style.*

below the waterline in the bows; early in the ship's life a benefactor donated a comprehensive range of fitness training equipment for the use of the ship's company, which is now available for use at any time of the day or night. The benefactor was Sir Donald Gosling, who founded the *Ark Royal Welfare Trust* and became its patron. Through the Trust, all kinds of improvements have been made to the living conditions and recreational facilities of the ship's company, from pictures and bunk-curtains in every messdeck, to sub-aqua equipment, to hiring English speaking guides for coach trips in foreign parts.

In his cabin on 3 deck directly above the keep fit training, the Chaplain is discussing with a rating their plans for a baptism to be performed on board when the ship returns to Portsmouth. The service will be held in the ship's Church in 7T, which has an altar at one end and a chalkboard at the other; this compartment doubles as a schoolroom where an officer of the Instructor specialisation is teaching Maths to a class of young ratings who wish to improve their grade in order to be eligible for advancement to the next higher rank. O-level tuition can also be provided for candidates for promotion to officer from the lower deck. Some ratings invest wisely in their spare time by following educational correspondence courses up to and including Open University degrees.

The senior Lieutenant Commander is chairing a weekly 'DOHDs' meeting in the Wardroom Guest Room. Using the ship's outline programme for the next fortnight as a starting point, the Deputy Heads of Department, Operations Officer and Commander's Assistant discuss each commitment in detail. Their task is to produce a minute by minute programme for the whole ship ensuring that conflicting activities are not planned to take place at the same time. A decision has just been reached on when to schedule a balloon tracking serial, which is needed to calibrate one of the missile tracking radars, but which will mean that the ship's freedom to manoeuvre will be restricted for one hour. Although the DHODs collectively have the resources of about 1000 men at their disposal, elaborate planning often has to be exercised if adequate manpower is to be available to meet the programme without prejudicing essential routine work. Similarly, care is needed to avoid inadvertently planning a conflict of activities; thus after a few moments' further discussion, training of the ceremonial Guard in the hangar is delayed by a day to let the fresh paint on the deck dry.

The DHODs disperse to brief their own departmental officers on their commitments in the next few days. Meanwhile the Whole Ship Coordinator, an experienced Warrant Officer, meets with Departmental Coordinators to add further detail to the programme which has just been agreed. The result is

*The Royal Guard is drilled in the hangar in preparation for a visit by Her Majesty Queen Elizabeth The Queen Mother—the ship's sponsor.*

published each evening in Daily Orders. These are a timetable of the next day's events complete with the names of ratings who have been nominated to carry out 'whole ship' tasks such as embarking ammunition. If a team of 20 ratings is needed for an activity, the rule is that each Coordinator has to nominate a certain number of his men in proportion to the size of his Department. In the same spirit of fairness, enormous care went into allocating which Departments are responsible for cleaning communal areas such as passageways and ladders used by all.

There are some tasks which cannot be planned, but have to be undertaken as and when an opportunity occurs; to fulfil these there are on-call groups of sailors based on a previously agreed departmental composition, available to turn out at any time of the day or night. Typically they may be needed for a Replenishment at Sea; or to tackle an incident such as a fire or flood. The ship's emergency team is exercised frequently and is occasionally required in earnest. Such is the speed of response that the very few incidents that do occur are dealt with before they can become serious.

Loudspeakers throughout the ship suddenly announce: ''Gash may now be ditched. Force H close up!'' The Officer of the Watch has taken advantage of the pause in the flying programme to allow departments to dispose of their rubbish. This is one of the permanent problems of the ship, because rubbish cannot

*A small 'whole ship' working party handling a load on the jetty at Gibraltar.*

*The ship's sponsor—Queen Elizabeth The Queen Mother at the Commissioning Ceremony.*

*Peter Nash, the President of Barclays Bank's North America's National Division, climbs out of a Sea King helicopter during a visit to the ship.*

be thrown over the side while the ship is close to a coast, nor when aircraft are operating in case some is sucked into the engines. A small mountain of sacks containing waste paper, used packing materials, galley waste and all kinds of other rubbish generated by a community of 1200 people soon accumulates, in a compartment set aside for the purpose. When the order to ditch gash is heard on the main broadcast, a dozen sailors nominated for the day from all departments and nicknamed 'Force H' (for no very good reason other than the wartime HMS *Ark Royal* formed part of the famous Mediterranean Force H until she was torpedoed in November 1941) gather in the starboard boat bay to clear out the gash compart-

ment and throw the sacks over the side. Equipment is being procured which will effectively treat the ship's rubbish so that in future it can be disposed of below the waterline without having to wait for a break in the flying programme, and in such a way that it will quickly degrade—and remove the thankless chore of gash ditching.

The Supply Commander is busy at his monthly task of counting money in the Cash Office on 5 deck. The ship's company are no longer paid cash-in-hand, but instead have their pay credited direct to their banks from a central computer at HMS *Centurion* in Gosport, Hampshire. Nevertheless if the ship is away from home for a long period, hundreds of thousands of pounds have to be

*The Supply Commander gets ready to count the cash—but looks as though he would prefer to spend it.*

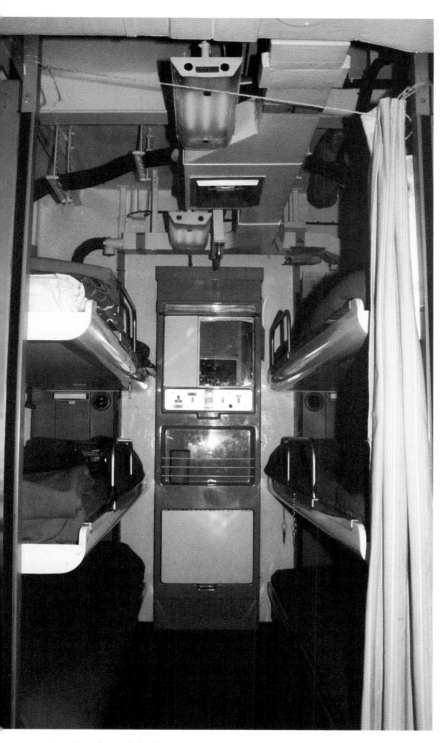

*A section of messdeck sleeping accommodation with six bunks in 3 tiers.*

carried in several different currencies to meet the sailors' requirements for cash and to pay the bills for stores and services incurred during foreign visits. The Cash Officer accounts for the public money in his charge to the last penny and each month balances his books and presents the cash to the Commander (S) for checking. Considering the huge number of transactions involved in providing a cheque-cashing and currency-changing service to the whole ship's company, producing a balance accurate to the last penny is no easy task. Very occasionally the Cash Officer does make a mistake; then the rule is quite clear—he makes up the difference out of his own pocket.

After Commander (S) has satisfied himself all the money is there, he departs to put the accounts in the next mail for further verification in the Ministry of Defence. Another visitor arrives for the Cash Officer. This is a young rating, recently married and sinking rapidly into debt because of easy credit offered nearly everywhere he looks. At the end of the day an individual's debts are not the Navy's problem; however the investment of a little expert advice will in this case lead to a rating with his mind on his job instead of worrying how his wife is going to pay the electricity bill.

A few compartments away on the same deck a Chief Petty Officer Stores Accountant is checking discrepancies between what the shore Stores organisation's computer thinks was sent to *Ark Royal* last month, and what the ship's stores computer thinks it has received. Led by a specialist officer, *Ark*'s stores team looks after an inventory of nearly 70,000 different items with a value of roughly £10,000,000. They range from nuts and bolts of every conceivable size, to very expensive electronic spares; whatever is needed to maintain the material efficiency of the ship can be located in one of the sixteen store-rooms in minutes, and if an urgently required item is not held on board, arrangements can be made for it to be delivered to the ship anywhere in the world in a remarkably short

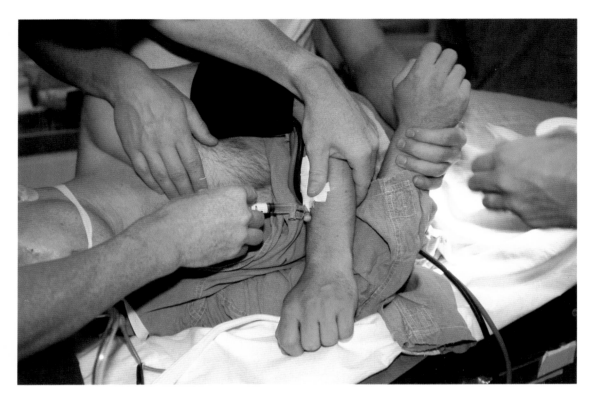

*Helping hands. A patient is brought round after an operation in the Sick Bay.*

time. The record was the arrival of a vital spare for the satellite communications equipment being received on board in New York less than 24 hours after a signal was sent demanding it. It crossed the Atlantic on Concorde. As with the taxpayer's money in the charge of the Cash Officer, stores are subject to rigorous accounting procedures and regular checks both by the ship's staff and by external auditors. Anyone who carelessly losses an item of stores on his personal charge is liable to have to repay the cost to the Crown—and that includes the Stores Officer.

Next door to the Stores Office is the Regulating Office. This is the domain of the Warrant Officer Master at Arms and his small team of Regulators, who are the ship's police force. Much of their work is administrative, such as keeping track of the regular stream of ratings being drafted to and from the ship, allocating them to messdecks, and making out leave passes and travel warrants. Aside from this routine work, the Warrant Officer Master at Arms's primary rôle is the maintenance of naval discipline and high standards of conduct in the ship. Through constant contact with the ship's company he is also able to act as a sounding board of morale. During *Ark Royal*'s first foreign visit, which was to Marseilles in November 1985 for four days, there was not a single disciplinary incident. A few weeks later when *Ark* gave shore leave in Crete, a Leading Cook did appear at the Commander's Table as a defaulter. He had returned to the jetty to wait for next liberty-boat back on board, and was invited for some drinks on a small ship there. He fell asleep, which was a pity because the ship was in fact a ferry, and much to his surprise he woke up in Athens.

One of the Leading Regulators is the ship's postman. 'Postie' is a very important person, for nothing lifts morale as much as the pipe "Mail is now ready for collection" made after weeks' worth of letters have arrived in a mountain of mailbags and been sorted for distribution to messdecks. Equally, a definite sadness can spread round the ship on the rare occasions when a consignment of mail fails to appear when expected. With the dedicated assistance of the Forces Mail Office at Mill Hill in London, 'Postie' has always succeeded in tracing missing mail and having it re-routed to catch up with the ship.

High and low throughout the ship, other tasks are being undertaken with quiet professionalism. The ship's surgical team is midway through an operation in the Sick Bay for removal of an appendix. Officers under Training are being instructed in Replenishment at Sea techniques by the Chief Boatswain's Mate. The Intelligence Officer is compiling the evening brief for the Admiral and his staff. Air Engineering specialists are testing a Sea Harrier's radio that they have stripped and repaired before replacing it in the aircraft. Details of a rating's eligibility for advancement are being verified in the Ship's Office before being included in the list for Captain's Requestmen. The Captain's Secretary is checking official mail before it is placed in files and circulated for action. The Navigator's Yeoman is making minutely accurate amendments to charts from the latest list of corrections. The Confidential Books Officer is recording receipt of the latest batch of cipher codes before signing them over to the Communications Officer. A Petty Officer Steward is calculating what wines and spirits will be needed for the official cocktail party at the next foreign port. A small team of volunteers is setting up the Closed Circuit television studio for the next programme. The Ship's Photographer is printing a set of pictures for the Public Relations Officer. A Cook is taking provisions to the Aircrew Refreshment Bar for tonight's flying meals. A Marine Engineering Mechanic is dipping fuel tanks to check fuel remaining. The Damage Control Officer and his assistant are planning a full-scale fire-fighting exercise.

The ship never sleeps.

*Families day. Ships allocate one day in the year, if possible, to take families to sea. With 3,000 guests on board,* Ark Royal *sails past HMS* Illustrious *out of Portsmouth Harbour.*

# CHAPTER FOUR

# PURPOSE

By any measure, HMS *Ark Royal* is expensive. The outlay of over £200,000,000 to build the ship is complete, but running costs will continue into the 21st century. Fuel, provisions, spares, updating of aircraft, weapon and sensor capabilities, maintenance, refits and manpower are very expensive commitments. Whereas the foregoing chapters give an insight into everyday activities on board, it is more than reasonable to ask, 'What is it all for?'

The Royal Navy's most important rôle in the nation's Defence Policy is nuclear deterrence. This task is currently performed by the four Polaris submarines of the 10th Submarine Squadron based at Faslane in Scotland. Massive civil engineering projects are being undertaken there in preparation for the arrival of four Trident submarines, of which the first (HMS *Vanguard*) is currently under construction at the Vickers shipyard in Barrow-on-Furness. Obtuse though it may seem, the object of spending so much money on an up-to-date nuclear capability is to reduce the possibility of ever having to fire a missile in anger; while at the same time providing a surer guard of the country's security because the missiles are somewhere at sea, always ready.

Since national security may be threatened at a level lower than one which requires nuclear response, conventional forces are still necessary to deter, or if necessary overcome, lesser ventures. Invasion of Southern, Central or Northern Europe by Warsaw Pact countries would immediately create a need for massive reinforcement of NATO forces. Men can be moved by air, but fuel, munitions and equipment would have to be brought in by sea. If the Atlantic was not open to reinforcement shipping, the war on land could be won in a few days—and not by NATO. The ability to deny access to the Atlantic to the Soviet Northern Fleet's ships and submarines is a vital part of NATO strategy. This is where *Ark Royal* fits in.

Like most of the Royal Navy's ships and submarines, *Ark Royal* is allocated to NATO in time of war and would operate under the ultimate control of the Supreme Allied Commander Atlantic (SACLANT), an American Admiral whose headquarters are at Norfolk, Virginia. One of SACLANT's subordinate Admirals is the NATO Commander of the Anti-Submarine Warfare Strike Force (COMASWSTRIKFOR in 'NATO-speak'). This post is filled by a Royal Naval Admiral, Flag Officer Flotilla Three (FOF3). In time of tension he would be embarked in *Ark Royal* or one of her sister ships, *Illustrious* or *Invincible*, controlling a force of ships with the task of closing the 'gaps' between Greenland, Iceland, the Faroes and Scotland to Soviet naval forces. Alternatively the force could be used by SACLANT to provide distant anti-submarine support to a United States Carrier Battle Group operating forward in the Norwegian Sea close to the Russian bases near North Cape.

No-one in the Royal Navy is under the illusion that war is anything but awful. All in *Ark Royal* are ready to play their part if called upon to do so, but they would much rather the need never arose. So far as *Ark Royal* is concerned, the best means of preventing this is to be good at sinking submarines in the North Atlantic—and being seen to be good. Operational efficiency depends of the successful combination of a wide range of professional skills in all departments on board, and can only be maintained by constant practice. It is hard enough for each individual to become proficient; harder for the whole team to work efficiently; even harder for a group of RN ships to operate well together; harder still for a group of ships from several countries to combine as a well-trained force. The answer is regular training.

*''Hands to Action Stations! Hands to Action Staions! Assume NBCD State 1, Condition Zulu!''* At 0830 one Friday the main broadcast summoned the ship's company to their stations, and *Ark Royal* sailed into the Atlantic from the U.S. Naval Base at Norfolk, fully closed up and secured for action, ready for the first stage of Exercise NORTHERN WEDDING. Shortly before lunch the state of readiness was reduced to Defence Watches, in which all departments are manned and operated 24 hours a day and are ready to resume Action Stations at a moment's notice. Five weeks later in the North Sea, the ship's company relaxed to normal sea routine and prepared to enter Amsterdam where the post-exercise discussions were to take place.

NORTHERN WEDDING was one of the largest NATO exercises to have been staged for many years. Starting with a preliminary working up phase for 'Blue' (friendly) forces in the Western Atlantic, it progressed to a silent passage across to the Norwegian Sea employing deceptive measures designed to

*Personnel of the damage control centre monitor progress in a full-scale firefighting exercise.*

*The submersible unit of an anti-submarine Sea King's Sonar System being winched back into the aircraft. The aircraft will then move to a new sector and resume its search for submarines.*

confuse the opposing 'Orange' (enemy) forces as to the intentions of the group. There followed an extended period providing seaward anti-submarine cover to the nuclear-powered aircraft-carrier USS *Nimitz* and her consorts close to the Norwegian coast; finally distant support was given to an amphibious landing group composed of ships from several nations. Peacetime air safety rules imposes a small but unavoidable degree of constraint on attacks between 'Orange' and 'Blue' forces; nevertheless prolonged operations such as NORTHERN WEDDING give invaluable experience, particularly in the important areas of logistics, communications and passing swift and accurate target information between widely dispersed ships of different Navies. The whole exercise was subsequently analysed in detail, and the lessons learned will eventually be incorporated into operational procedures.

Just as important were the political messages signalled by the United States' demonstration of willingess to commit major units to operations in close proximity to the Soviet home base. NORTHERN WEDDING was closely monitored by Soviet forces, and in 1987 officers of several nations, including the U.S.S.R., were given facilities to witness Exercise PURPLE WARRIOR at first hand under the (then) recent Stockholm agreement. Additionally, NATO cohesion was nurtured by European countries contributing forces at the sort of level expected by the United States to match their own substantial commitment to the defence of Europe.

While *Ark Royal* was participating with other forces in air defence and anti-submarine operations, the opportunity was taken to organise internal exercises. One important consideration when the ship is under prolonged threat of attack is how to feed the ship's company without reducing readiness for action below an acceptable level. 'Action Messing' is the solution. Each part of the ship sends one sixth of its action crew away to the dining-halls at a time; there they eat a hot meal as quickly as possible and return to their station to allow the next man to do the same. This way the whole ship's company can eat a square meal in 45 minutes. If the degree of threat is too great to allow even a one sixth relaxation in readiness, and alternative is to activate the complex 'Action Snacks' organisation. Under this system the galley and dining-hall crew deliver urns of hot drink and sacks of food to pre-determined positions around the ship, known as 'countries'. Each sack contains a certain number of packed meals. The food in the sacks is of the sort that does not make crumbs that might get into computer keyboards. 'Prime Ministers' distribute the snacks around their countries, and whole ship's company gets something to keep them going at their Action Station until there is a chance of a proper meal.

War is said to be 99% boredom and 1% terror. Certainly a consideration in peacetime exercises is how to occupy the ship's company closed up at Action Stations if nothing is happening. Here is a tailor-made chance to run Damage Control exercises, which otherwise are a major interruption to normal business. Working from a carefully planned scenario and timetable, 'damage' will be inflicted at several points in the ship by a small team of 'wreckers'. The first that the unsuspecting occupants of a compartment know of their involvement is a wrecker setting off a thunderflash and smoke canister in their midst and standing back to see what they do about it. What they should do is inform the Damage Control centre (called HQ1) what has happened and attempt to put the 'fire' out with nearby appliances. Reactions can be confused by a realistically made up 'casualty' rushing in with blood pouring from a metal splinter sticking out of his head. The wrecker, now an umpire, decides that the fire is out of control and the battle is now on to contain the incident from spreading to neighbouring compartments. An hour later the ship is full of smoke and water, and while blackened and exhausted firefighters start to clear up, a de-brief dissects the exercise to

A ''wrecker'' sets off a smoke canister while firefighters are briefed. The leader of the firesuitmen wears a radio strapped to his breathing apparatus.

The firefighting team searches a smoke-filled compartment for casualties.

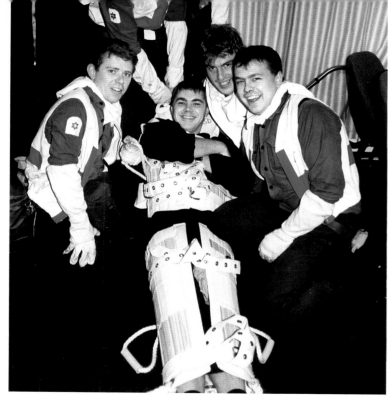

*A 'casualty' in a Neil Robertson stretcher looks relieved to have survived the exercise.*

*The ship's company is prepared for every eventuality. Operational training at Portland includes practice in disaster relief.*

*Provisions are loaded on board at Portsmouth shortly before deploying.*

*On return to harbour, an unserviceable Sea King is craned ashore to be repaired and returned to front line service.*

discover what went well and what needs to be done better next time.

*Ark Royal* returned to Portsmouth 43 days after sailing from Virginia. She had just 15 days to carry out essential maintenance, restore and give a week's Summer leave to all the ship's company before sailing again on Exercise AUTUMN TRAIN. This was a purely national exercise; participating ships gathered en route to Gibraltar and included some setting off for Gulf and Falklands patrols. After a fortnight's concentrated exercises the force entered Gibraltar. Immediately *Ark Royal* was invaded by Granada Television crews, who with the help of the ship's company made ready for the filming of a 'Rock Spectacular'. This demanded detailed organisation which had started some months earlier, and on Sunday 26th October Gibraltar harbour throbbed to the sounds of Bob Geldof, Cindy Lauper, Alison Moyet and Paul Young for a programme to be transmitted on all ITV stations on Christmas Day. Filming stopped at 1800. The stages and equipment were dismantled through the night, and at 0630 *Ark Royal* sailed for Lisbon

*Rock Spectacular. Bob Geldof in concert on board in Gibraltar.*

*Cleared to land.*

**Opposite:** *Four ''sticks'' of Marines ascend to the flight deck on the forward aircraft lift.*

*Royal Netherlands Marines embark in a Commando Sea King of 845 Squadron.*

*Dawn, and the 'enemy' coast is on the horizon.*

for a goodwill visit and a few day's rest.

Eleven days later *Ark Royal* manoeuvred in the confined waters of the Firth of Clyde while the Mark 4 Sea Kings of 845 Squadron ferried 400 men of the Royal Netherlands Marine Corps on board. This was the beginning of the ship's 'Amphibious Work Up', again the result of several months' planning. A few days earlier 820 Squadron had disembarked off the Cornish coast, airlifting its personnel and equipment and being replaced by the men and aircraft of 845 Squadron—a major organisational task in itself. By the time the Dutch Marines embarked, all unused deck space within the ship had been identified and allocated for them to sleep on; ammunition and weapon stowages were set aside; guides were detailed to help the Marines find their way about, and 'assault routes' were clearly marked out within the ship. Having completed a slow-time landing rehearsal, *Ark Royal* sailed round the North of Scotland to avoid some bad weather and executed an airborne amphibious landing of the whole force of Marines and their equip-

ment near Arbroath. After collecting them again, *Ark Royal* moved to the Netherlands coast and finally disembarked her guests to Valkenburg Air Force Base. In ten days a welcome spirit of comradeship and efficient cooperation had been formed.

In the preceding three months *Ark Royal* had taken part in an RN training period and a major NATO exercise and had benefitted from the very valuable experience of multiship, multi-national and tri-Service operations. Additionally the ship and her men would be seen by a television audience of millions on Christmas afternoon.

Maintaining a favourable public awareness of the Royal Navy is seen as a highly important function involving everyone. There is something about 'Ark Royal' which attracts public interest, and which has been a peculiar asset of ships of that famous name ever since the commissioning in 1938 of the Royal Navy's first purpose-built major aircraft-carrier. She was the third HMS *Ark Royal*, and the spirit continues to this day in the fifth ship to bear the name.

*Dress rehearsal for the ship's Volunteer Band. Under the direction of a Royal Marines Band Colour Sergeant, many of the ship's company learned to play a musical instrument from scratch. Within a year the Band had reached a sufficiently high standard to Beat Retreat during high profile foreign visits.*

*Ark Royal* navigates the Thames Barrier in June 1987 for her first visit to London.

*Old and new—the* Ark *passes the* Cutty Sark *prior to mooring at Greenwich.*

*4th July,
1986—Independence
Day fireworks in New
York harbour.*

*The ship with the
island floodlit,
berthed at Fort
Lauderdale.*

There are tens of thousands of visitors to the new *Ark Royal* every year. Each one is treated as an important person, who should leave with a lasting impression of a welcoming and efficient ship. The favourite visitor of all is Queen Elizabeth The Queen Mother; Her Majesty launched and commissioned both the fourth and the fifth HMS *Ark Royal*, and has maintained the connection by visiting and meeting the ship's company on several occasions.

*Ark*'s first commitment on becoming operational in 1986 was to project the image of the Royal Navy in New York during the centennial celebrations of the Statue of Liberty. Thus the deployment which culminated in Exercise NORTHERN WEDDING started on 17th June, when families gathered to wave the ship off for 3½ months. On 3rd July *Ark Royal* and the frigates *Sirius* and *Cleopatra* took their places in a column of 40 ships from all over the world for a ceremonial entry into New York Harbour. *Ark*'s anchorage was on the Bay Ridge Flats a short distance from Queen Elizabeth 2, and with a prime view of the Statue of Liberty and the inspiring Manhattan skyline. Flag Officer Flotilla Three entertained a party of guests including US Secretary of Defense and the British Ambassador to dinner in the Admiral's Dining Cabin in the evening. At 2130 a spectacular light display heralded the unveiling by President Reagan of the restored Statue of Liberty.

The main events of Independence Day were a review of the assembled international Fleet by President Reagan steaming past on board the battleship USS *Iowa*, followed by a parade of tall ships making their way up harbour through a throng of thousands of small craft out on the Hudson River. In the evening a colossal, synchronised firework

Ark Royal *enters Fort Lauderdale, Florida in August 1986.*

*HMS* Ark Royal *sails from New York.*

display took place along the Manhattan waterfront and around the Statue of Liberty. When the last salvo of fireworks finally expired, darkness fell over the fleet and the senses were left numbed. As though at a signal, the thousands of small boats from which people had been watching turned and made their way out to sea, so that the entire harbour seemed to be a moving river of navigation lights.

However the show had been stolen earlier in the day by *Ark Royal*. The first event of the morning had been the launch of a pair of Sea Harriers in the harbour. They flew up river to the East Side of New York, turned over USS *Iowa* and came back towards the Statue of Liberty. Descending to 100 feet, they slowed to a hover, turned towards the Statue, and bowed. The Royal Navy's salute to the USA's most treasured national symbol was shown on television news across the country on five successive evenings.

*Ark Royal* and her men earn their keep.

Opposite: *Launch of a Sea Harrier from the ship anchored in New York harbour.*

*Sea Harriers against the New York skyline.*

*Officers and men of
820 squadron
preparing for a group
photograph.*

*One of the squadrons
prepare for a family
picture.*

*HMS* York *Lynx helicopter, fitted with two Sea Skua missiles and a surveillance pod, overflies* Ark Royal.